I Got Time Today!

Put an End to Writer's Block
--One Prompt a Time.

AfroSoFly

I Got Time Today!

Put an End to Writer's Block--One Prompt at a Time

By

Dominique D. Glisson

Founder and CEO of AfroSoFly Inc.

COPYRIGHT ©2022 AFROSOFLY PUBLISHING, LLC

ALL RIGHTS RESERVED

All rights reserved. No part of this publication may be reproduced, distributed, or transmitted in any form or by any means, including photocopying, recording, or other electronic or mechanical methods, without the prior written permission of the publisher, except in the case of brief quotations embodied in critical reviews and certain other noncommercial uses permitted by copyright law. For permission requests, contact the publisher at the email below.

Ordering Information:

Special discounts are available on quantity purchases by corporations, associations and others. For details, contact the publisher at the email address below.

AFROSOFLY PUBLISHING, LLC

info@afrosofly.com

www.afrosofly.com

ISBN
978-1-7349245-4-1

Just Write

Writer's Block is a temporary condition (regardless of how permanent it feels) that many writers struggle with. It is the mere act of flexing our fingers to write or type something great and nothing comes out. But it's not just that right?

There's also the pressure to produce because WE ARE WRITERS. It's legit what we were born to do. Alas, the struggle is real. That's where prompt writing comes in handy!

Prompt writing is not about perfection--or even complete thoughts. It's about free writing whatever comes to mind with the influence of a particular prompt. Release the need to be a perfect writer and JUST WRITE.

If you are committed to defeating Writer's Block, flex your fingers and shout:
I GOT TIME TODAY!

✿ Challenge ✿

Set a timer for 5 minutes and write uninterrupted for each prompt.

AfroSoFly

Share your progress with us! Use the #AfroSoFlyJournal hashtag on Twitter, Instagram, Facebook or TikTok.

Subscribe to AfroSoFly.com to receive exclusive offers and more!

I Feel Most in Love With Myself When...
● ● ●

Fill the Empty Walls
•••

12 Six-Minute Videos

Smile at the Wind
•••

Depths of Wisdom
• • •

Coffee, Tea and Whiskey
•••

Into Some Nasty Business
•••

Even with Only $6 in My Bank Account
•••

Creep Through a Windshield

I've Earned My Place in This House
• • •

Even Better Conversation

• • •

Unwanted Trigger
...

Too Old to Still Be Going Through This
• • •

Fruit Juice and Red Wine
...

Healthy as Can Be

Focused on the Wrong Shit
...

Too Young to Remember
•••

Astronomical Interest
• • •

Forced Her Hand

Kinks in My Head

Bigotry in the Air

Cash, Card or Crypto
• • •

A Word from a Drunk
...

Become the Whole Package
•••

Snored Like an Saint
• • •

Sex as a Solution

The Most High Forgave Him
•••

Lost and Never Found
...

A Heroine's Prayer
• • •

I Want You to Feel Uncomfortable

•••

Flip Phones and Lubrication

Stolen Lobster Tails

Think I'm Ain't?
• • •

Not Diplomatic Enough

30 Shades of Brown
• • •

My Spirit Said...

Secret Secretions

Nickel in the Snow
•••

Fuck You, In Advance
•••

Clusters of Confusion

The Presence of the Past

...

Peaches, Apples and Poker
• • •

Generated on Sunday

Invisible Barriers

By Appointment Only
...

Purple Sunglasses on the Nightstand
• • •

The Sake of Our Nation
• • •

Keep Art Real

Uncovered Conspiracy
• • •

Red to Black

•••

Chocolate Covered Dandelions

•••

I Stopped Explaining Myself When...
•••

Pause
...

Your Message Matters

A New Name
•••

Raw Fruit Crepes

•••

Turn Signal

•••

Lunch and Laughter

The Place on Tompkins

Brownstone in Nairobi
• • •

A Child at This Age
• • •

The Same but Different
•••

Victims of White Supremacy
• • •

The Five-Letter Word
•••

Can't Be Reasoned With

•••

Personal Receipts
●●●

The Man Behind the Man
•••

Kangaroo's Goose
•••

Too Close to the Hole

Daddy's Nurse
•••

Vaginal Power
• • •

Dysfunctional Peace
•••

That's Love?
•••

Brown Image on the Cover

• • •

Scattered Brain

Civilized Savagery
•••

Deemed to Be Dope

...

More from The Author

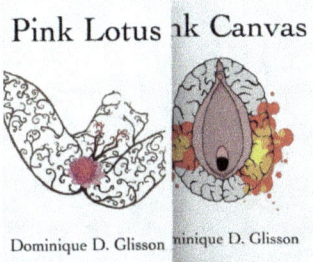

Pink Canvas
A collection of poems written for any woman seeking love through her reproductive organs. Pink Canvas vividly captures the thoughts of a woman battling with vaginal power, seduction, lust, love, abstinence and self-worth.

Pink Lotus
A collection of poems written for the healing process of any woman who has her vagina in her heart's position. Developed from Pink Canvas, Pink Lotus continues the journey toward vaginal power, seduction and self-worth.

Keep a look out for the third and final installment of the Pink Trilogy by Dominique D. Glisson-- coming November 2022!

AfroSoFly.com

AfroSoFly

www.ingramcontent.com/pod-product-compliance
Lightning Source LLC
Chambersburg PA
CBHW071913070526
44583CB00016B/1967